SMART AS HELL
ADVICE

A Year's Worth of Wisdom For Goal Achievement and Success

By Glenn Hughes

Find us on the web at *SMARTasHell.com*.

To report errors, please send a note to *info@smartashell.com*.

Notice of Rights
COPYRIGHT © 2015 by SMART as Hell. All rights reserved. No part of this book may be reproduced or transmitted in any form by any means, electronic, mechanical, photocopying, recording, or otherwise, without the prior written permission of the publisher.

ISBN: 978-0-9894655-3-3
LCCN: 2015914743
Oct 10, 2015

For information on getting permission for reprints and excerpts, contact *info@smartashell.com*.

Notice of Liability
The information in this book is distributed on an "As Is" basis without warranty. While every precaution has been taken in the preparation of the book, neither the author nor the Publisher shall have any liability to any person or entity with respect to any loss or damage caused or alleged to be caused directly or indirectly by the instructions contained in this book.

SAH Publishing
San Jose, California, USA

Thanks

- To Dad for instilling in me a love for reading.
- To Angie for encouraging all of my varied interests.
- To my high school teacher, Mrs. Remington, who often said, "It's a sad day that you don't learn something new".
- And – of course – to those who wrote or spoke the wisdom contained in these pages. Hopefully, these words inspire you as much as they have me.

Contents

Objectives   VII

Foreword by Brent Bloom   IX

Part One: About   1

Part Two: Activities   9

Part Three: Advice   27

Part Four: Resources   133

Find supplemental videos, worksheets, and links at:

http://smartashell.com/blog/SAHAdvice

Objectives

After reading *SMART as Hell Advice*, readers will be able to create, question, and calibrate a meaningful personal or professional goal.

PART ONE

At the end of Part One, readers will be able to:
- Define the SMART acronym
- Identify 13 applications for SMART goals

PART TWO

At the end of Part Two, readers will be able to:
- Identify eight exercises to improve their goals
- Apply eight exercises to improve their goals

PART THREE

At the end of Part Three, readers will be able to:
- Improve their goals, using more than 300 'words of wisdom'
- Challenge their goals, using more than 300 reflection questions

Foreword

What the hell… That was the first thing that came to my mind when I was asked to write the foreword to **SMART as Hell Advice**. You see, I've had a little advanced notice regarding some of the notable people that agreed to write forewords for Glenn's SMART as Hell® book series. The list is laden with legends and gurus from the worlds of Learning & Development (L&D), Organizational Development, and Communications. All are authors themselves and most are award winners. So again, what the hell…

Well, hold on… let me do a quick process check… I may be coming down a little hard on myself. The one thing I have over all the sages referenced above is the fact that I've known Glenn since 1987.

Our relationship was forged in the Silicon Valley trenches, battling with bits, bytes, and logic analyzers. Yes, at the core of it all, Glenn and I are a couple of engineers who shifted our troubleshooting skills from solving hardware & software problems to solving people problems. We both migrated, years ago, to a talent management team where we *accelerated learning*. That was our mission, and I'd say we did one hell of a job.

Our team took a small, yet highly skilled, group of engineers and L&D practitioners and established a Hall of Fame operation, as determined by *TRAINING Magazine*. We were not only on par with the likes of IBM, Microsoft, Verizon, Ernst & Young, and Ritz Carlton, we were amongst the first to be honored as *TRAINING* Hall of Famers. So, when it comes to solving people problems, Glenn knows what the hell he's talking about.

The bottom line is that Glenn really is SMART as Hell. I don't say that about many people. And I certainly don't say it out loud. For example, I would include Ed and Mike in my Top Five SMART as Hell list, but you won't find their last names in this foreword since I know you would try to poach them from my inner circle. Glenn, on the other hand, has already plastered his last name all over this book, so that cat is out of the bag. Now his genius is available for all to use. It's at your fingertips; it's within eyesight; and it's within hearing distance, depending on which format of this book you've gained access to.

SMART as Hell Advice is brilliant in its simplicity and application. The book is filled with words of wisdom, quotes, proverbs, axioms, and the like, which are tested, manipulated, and discussed via activities that are masterfully laid out for the reader. The outputs and insights gained from these activities will vary from reader to reader and from novice facilitators to master facilitators, but one thing is safe to say… a deeper exploration of goals, both personal and professional, will be enabled.

For those of us striving to create and enhance high performing teams, Glenn has added a fantastic set of tools to our arsenal, assuming we apply what is taught in **SMART as Hell Advice.**

Final note… if my charming, light-hearted wit and humor did not come across in this foreword, then chances are that Glenn edited my words. This, I'm afraid, is out of my control; however, for those of you taking the time, the decision to read this book and apply it is yours and is completely within your control! To that end, let me leave you with a quote from Jim Rohn: "My suggestion would be to walk away from the 90% who don't and join the 10% who do."

Brent Bloom
Vice President of Central Operations in AGS (Applied Global Support), at Applied Materials Inc.

Brent is a Talent Management expert with extensive leadership experience driving Learning & Development, Organizational Design, Organizational Development, Talent Acquisition, Change Management, and Team Facilitation.

Part One

About Smart as Hell Advice

SMART AS HELL ADVICE: AN INTRODUCTION

Welcome to SMART as Hell Advice

WHAT IS THIS BOOK ABOUT?

SMART as Hell Advice is a one-year collection of provocations. These quotations, proverbs, maxims, mantras, mottos, axioms, beliefs, morals, tenets, adages, fortune cookie sayings, and words of wisdom are here to inspire your reflection, action, and achievement. Use this world-class advice to create, question, and calibrate your life goals.

WHY DID I WRITE THIS BOOK?

I love proverbs and quotations. I collect them. I read them. I digest them. I argue with them. I test them. Most importantly, I return to them. Often.

I use quotations repeatedly in my speeches, in my workshops, in my coaching, and in my writing. Yet no matter how many times I read, hear, or share a line like, "Progress has little to do with speed, but much to do with direction", I never tire of it. In fact, every time I hear such a maxim, I hear it anew, in the context of that day, that place, that audience.

These words of advice provide a lens on life. Some quotes view life through a wide-angle lens. Some provide a close-up. Most articulate a basic truth that we couldn't express without the author's help.

Quotations and proverbs cut like a knife through the lazy language of our lives. They are an antidote to bloated paragraphs and the only productive response to self-obsessed tweets. They stand self-contained; they stand the test of time; and – most importantly – they take a stand.

While that explains why I love quotations, it does not explain why I wrote this book. Let me try again. In 2008, I assessed over 30,000 goals from businesses, non-profit organizations, government agencies, and individuals. What did I learn? The vast majority of goals are awful: vague, lame, and irrelevant. In fact, most of the goals were counter-productive to what the goal-writer hoped to achieve.

Many of these came from the hands of people taught to write goals using the SMART acronym. SMART usually stands for Specific, Measureable, Attainable, Relevant, and Time-bound. The acronym has been around since the 1980's, but – judging from the goals I've assessed – the training doesn't work. In fact, surveys conducted by Gallup show that almost half of employees don't know what they are supposed to do at work.

This lack of clarity is unfortunate. It leads to misalignment, inefficiency, and frustration. And if we're that unclear in the modern workplace, imagine how we are in the rest of our lives.

As a result of these findings, I started *SMART as Hell®*, a project helping individuals consistently assess, write, and realize their goals. Over the past few years, I've presented tools such as the SMARTometer and the SMART Storyboard at conferences, webinars, and workshops across the country.

SMART as Hell Advice is the second in a series of *SMART as Hell* books that will make this research available to everyone. This book serves three purposes:

- *Inspire* readers to create meaningful personal goals
- *Provoke* readers to question their goals more deeply than they ever have before
- *Help* readers articulate and calibrate their goals in a way that enables success

If *SMART as Hell Advice* can deliver on these promises, I will consider it a success.

WHO AM I?

I'm Glenn Hughes. In my various roles as an engineer, manager, trainer, facilitator, and coach, I've accumulated years of experience helping individuals and teams improve their performance. I've published books, designed workshops, worked with big companies, and won multiple awards for my work. You can look me up on my website – *SMARTasHell.com* – or find me on LinkedIn to see what I've done lately.

Feel free to drop me a note and join my networks to start or continue a conversation.

WHO SHOULD READ THIS BOOK?

If you are interested in assessing, writing, and realizing your personal and professional goals – or helping others realize theirs, you should read – and use – SMART as Hell Advice.

The target audience for this book includes:

- ✓ Achievers
- ✓ Non-Achievers
- ✓ Dreamers
- ✓ Realists
- ✓ Students
- ✓ Athletes
- ✓ Parents
- ✓ Couples
- ✓ Managers
- ✓ Trainers
- ✓ Facilitators
- ✓ Coaches
- ✓ Teachers
- ✓ Human Resource Professionals
- ✓ Counselors
- ✓ Team Leaders
- ✓ Global Teams

WHAT IS "SMART AS HELL"?

The term *SMART as Hell*® applies to any goal, output, or product that fully meets the *SMART as Hell*® criteria – Specific, Measurable, Aggressively Attainable, Relevant, and Time-bound. Here are a number of examples:

- *Personal Goals*: Graduate with an MBA from State University with a 3.5 GPA or above within three years.
- *Health Goals*: Reduce my weight from 187 pounds to 170 pounds by June 15th.
- *Financial Goals*: Increase my credit score from 590 to 750 within two years.
- *Project Goals*: Receive customer sign-off for the Alpha project design by December 3rd.

- *Performance Reviews*: Increase product sales to Beta Electronics by 35% by end of the second quarter.
- *Products*: Design an automobile that travels 300 miles on a gallon of gas by 2020.
- *Meeting Outcomes*: The attendees will spend 15 minutes to reach a 'go/no go' decision on the proposed sales strategy.
- *Presentation 'Call to Action'*: Today, I would like you to approve $10,000 for the Alpha Project.
- *Deliverables*: Recruiting will forward 15 candidate resumes to Patty by noon, Friday.
- *Action Items*: Bob will email a first draft of the vendor agreement to Sandy by the end of Wednesday.
- *Training Objectives*: At the end of this training, you will be able to replace an oil filter correctly, in 20 minutes or less.
- *Problem Solving/Quality*: Decrease lost package rate from 2.1% to 1.0% or less by May 20th.
- *Coaching/Mentoring*: In the next 30 minutes, I'd like to identify two strategies for dealing with my difficult teammate.

CITATIONS

Citing quotations and 'words of wisdom' is a tricky endeavor. It's all too easy to find attributions on the internet. Unfortunately, most of the attributions lack proof and – subsequently – credibility.

I spent a significant amount of time researching these quotations. I only credit authors whose words I could source directly (in some cases, with a translator) or from a credible source (Yale or Oxford books of quotations, for example).

I've assigned attributions throughout *SMART as Hell Advice* as follows:
- Sourced from the author's book *(Mihaly Csikszentmihalyi, "Finding Flow")*

- Sourced from the author's article or paper *(Peter Drucker, 'Drucker on Managerial Change', Harvard Business Review)*
- Sourced from a translated book *(Confucius, "Analects", Trans. Hinton)*
- Sourced from a credible website *(Henry David Thoreau, walden.org)*
- Commonly attributed, but not validated *(Attributed to Arnold H. Glasgow)*
- Unknown *(Unknown)* or Various *(Various)*

If you are aware of a primary source for any of the attributed or unknown quotes, please contact me.

HOW SHOULD I USE THIS BOOK?

1. **Identify** a goal that you are working on.
2. **Choose** one of the activities from Part Two of this book.
3. **Choose** a piece of advice from Part Three of this book.
4. **Challenge** your goal using the activity and the advice.
5. **Download** the *SMART as Hell Advice Reflection Worksheet* at *SMARTasHell.com/blog/SAHAdvice* to dig deeper into any piece of advice while capturing your thoughts and actions.
6. **Watch** our videos at *http://YouTube.com/SMARTasHellVideo* for examples, instructions, and inspiration.

Have fun and please share your results with us.

Part Two

Smart as Hell Advice Activities

ACTIVITY 01
ONE A DAY / WEEK

This action-learning exercise from renowned learning expert Thiagi lasts up to a year (visit *thiagi.com* for more great interactive exercises). Implement one piece of practical advice each day or week – and learn from your experience.

PURPOSE: Apply and enhance one practical advice each day (or week).

TIME: 15 to 20 minutes each day of the week.

PREPARATION: Open the note-taking tool of your preference.

FLOW:

1. *Find your advice.* At the beginning of your day or week, choose a piece of advice from Part Three.
2. *Review the advice.* Translate the advice into a specific technique that you want to apply to your goal that day or week. Record the technique in your note-taking tool of your preference.
3. *Plan your application.* Ask yourself,
   - How many ways can I apply this technique?
   - What barriers might I encounter?
   - How will I measure my success?

   Record your responses and insights.
4. *Implement the technique.* Follow your plan, but be flexible for additional application opportunities.

5. ***Debrief each evening***. Reflect on the process and outcomes.
   - How did the technique work?
   - What were some unexpected results?
   - What did I learn about the technique?
   - How can I improve the technique to produce better results?
   - What should I do differently tomorrow?

   Record your responses and insights.

6. ***Score your performance each day***. How did I do?
   0) I ignored the technique.
   1) I applied the technique; reflected a little; learned nothing.
   2) I applied the technique, reflected, and learned something.
   3) I applied it, reflected, and learned something very useful.

7. ***Continue using the technique***. Incorporate the technique as part of your regular tool kit. Share it with others. Write a book!

8. ***Repeat***. Choose another piece of advice.

PLAY SAMPLE

- Pat selected Helen Keller's advice, "*Life is either a daring adventure or nothing.*" She decided to call one 'impossible' client each day.
- **Monday** - Pat made one call, but didn't reach the client. *1 point.*
- **Tuesday** - Pat was too busy to make calls. *0 points.*
- **Wednesday** – Pat reached two clients in the morning, learning that morning calls get a higher response. *2 points.*
- **Thursday** – Pat didn't reach any new clients. *1 point.*
- **Friday** – Two clients returned Pat's calls. Pat didn't make a sale but did learn important information about a competitor. *3 points.*
- **Saturday Reflection** – Pat believes that this technique is useful with perseverance. She will continue this practice in the coming year.

ACTIVITY 02
PROVERB PAIRS

The meaning of one sentence can change when a second sentence is added to it. Select two pieces of advice, pair them, and discover how they interact with each other.

PURPOSE: Strengthen your goal and plan by reflecting on two pieces of advice.

TIME: 5 minutes.

PREPARATION: None.

FLOW:

1. *Choose your advice.* Select a piece of advice from Part Three. Read and reflect on it.
2. *Choose another advice.* Read and reflect on it.
3. *Pair the advice.* Ask yourself,
    - Do these complement each other? How?
    - Do they build on each other? How?
    - Do they contradict each other? How?
    - Which should go first? Why? What if you change the order?

    Record your responses and insights.
4. *Implement the pair.* Use your insights to strengthen your goal or your plan.

PLAY SAMPLE

- Pat selected Helen Keller's advice, "*Life is either a daring adventure or nothing.*"
- Pat then selected, "*When you judge another, you do not define them, you define yourself.*"
- Pat decided that the two pieces of advice complement and build on each other. If Pat takes a series of risks, more conservative colleagues will probably judge her actions as 'risky' or 'stupid'. This might say more about their aversion to risk than it says about Pat's actions.
- Pat has resolved to listen to useful feedback. She will not, however, let negative judgment impact her resolve to accomplish her goals.

ACTIVITY 03
MAXIM MASH-UP

Combine two quotes to create one better, deeper sentence that is no longer than the longer of the two original sentences.

PURPOSE: Create a new maxim that you can apply to your goal.

TIME: 15 minutes.

PREPARATION: None.

FLOW:

1. *Choose your advice.* Select a piece of advice from Part Three. Read and reflect on it.
2. *Choose another piece of advice.* Read and reflect on it.
3. *Combine the advice.* Combine the two quotes to create one better, deeper sentence that is no longer than the longer of the two original sentences. If, for example, one quote is six words long and the other is nine words long, the new sentence should be nine words or less.
4. *Reflect on the new advice.* How does the advice change after being combined? Is the new advice stronger or weaker than the original advice? How?
5. *Implement the new advice.* Use the new insights to strengthen your goal or your plan.

PLAY SAMPLE

- Pat selected Helen Keller's advice, "*Life is either a daring adventure or nothing.*"
- Pat then selected, "*When you judge another, you do not define them, you define yourself.*"
- Pat combined the two pieces of advice to create a new sentence: "*When you define a daring adventure, you define yourself.*"
- Pat found this new maxim to be stronger than either of the original quotes. She is looking for a new project, so this new maxim applies directly to her situation.
- Based on this advice, Pat decided that her next project should redefine her personal brand.
- In the following 30 days, Pat will find a 'daring' project that will help her create a new personal brand.

ACTIVITY 04
VERSUS

Pick two quotes. Which better applies to your current goal?

PURPOSE: Compare two or more pieces of advice and then apply the best advice to your current goal.

TIME: 5 minutes.

PREPARATION: None.

FLOW:

1. *Choose your advice*. Select a piece of advice from Part Three. Read and reflect on it.
2. *Choose another piece of advice*. Read and reflect on it.
3. *Optionally, choose a third piece of advice*. Read and reflect on it.
4. *Compare the advice*. Consider how each piece of advice applies to your goal.
5. *Choose the best advice*. Which piece of advice most strongly and positively impacts your goal? How? Why?
6. *Implement the advice*. Use the most important insights to strengthen your goal or your plan.

PLAY SAMPLE

- Pat selected Helen Keller's advice, "*Life is either a daring adventure or nothing.*"
- Pat then selected the advice, "*When you judge another, you do not define them, you define yourself.*"
- Pat applied each piece of advice to her goal of "Increasing sales by 35% by Dec 31st."
- Pat felt that Helen Keller's advice best fit her goal. Her teammates think her goal is too aggressive, but she is tired of being an average salesperson.
- Pat decided that each week she will call five companies that have previously rejected her sales proposals.

ACTIVITY 05
PRONOUN PLAY

Change the pronouns of your advice and revisit the provocation question. No quote in this book is irrelevant if you approach it with the right perspective.

PURPOSE: Adapt the advice to be more relevant to your situation.

TIME: 5 minutes.

PREPARATION: None.

FLOW:

1. *Find your advice.* Select a piece of advice from Part Three. Read and reflect on it.
2. *Change the pronouns.*
    - Change 'your' to 'their' or 'your team'.
    - Change 'you' to 'they', 'them', or 'your team'.
    - Change 'us' to 'them'.
    - Change 'we' to 'you', 'I', or 'they'.
    - Change 'I' to 'they' or 'teams'.
    - Change 'man' to 'woman', 'you', 'your', or 'your team'.
    - Change 'people' to 'you' or 'your team'.
    - Change 'managers' to 'leaders' or 'people'.
    - Change 'employees' to 'students', 'people', or 'teams'.

3. *Reflect*. How does changing the pronouns change your perspective? Is the advice more relevant now? How?
4. *Apply the advice*. Use your new perspective to apply the advice.

PLAY SAMPLE

- Pat selected the advice, *"When you judge another, you do not define them, you define yourself."*
- Pat changed the pronouns to, *"When I judge another, I do not define them, I define myself"* and *"When my manager judges me, she does not define me, she defines herself."*
- Pat realized that recent feedback she gave her sister reflected her own values rather than the values of her sister. She took a note to approach her sister differently this week.
- Pat also noted that her manager provided negative feedback on her goal last week. Pat took the feedback very personally. Perhaps her manager's feedback doesn't define Pat, but just provides a useful perspective on her goal. Pat will revisit that conversation with her manager next week.

ACTIVITY 06
SMART GOAL PHOTO JOLT

From a collection of ten or more images, choose images that represent your goal and your advice.

PURPOSE: Use visualization techniques to strengthen your understanding of your goal and your commitment to your goal.

TIME: 10 minutes.

PREPARATION: Collect a set of metaphorical images. High quality image sets are available for purchase at *PhotoJolts.com*.

FLOW:

1. *Write your goal.* Write and review your current goal
2. *Choose the first photograph.* Select a photo that acts as a metaphor for your goal. With a partner, or in a journal, describe the image.
3. *Find your advice.* Select a piece of advice from Part Three. Read and reflect on it.
4. *Choose the second photograph.* Select a photo that acts as a metaphor for the advice you selected. With a partner, or in a journal, describe the image.
5. *Reflect.* What conclusions, insights, idea, or actions can you or your partner draw from the images you selected?

PLAY SAMPLE

- Pat's goal is to, "Make a sale to a large local company."
- Pat chose a skyscraper to symbolize her goal, saying, "This represents the large company I want to sell to."
- Pat selected Helen Keller's advice, "*Life is either a daring adventure or nothing.*"
- Pat then selected the dead fish image, saying, "This represents my daring adventure. I'll succeed or end up on the pile of all the salespeople who failed before me."
- Pat reflects, "The images give me a couple of ideas. The tower makes me think that perhaps I need to sell to an executive instead of a junior buyer. How can I make connections higher in the organization? The fish picture gives me two ideas. First, what bait can I offer the customer? Second, fish swim in schools to be safe. Maybe I should go in with a stronger team?"
- Pat decides she will meet with her colleagues to discuss alternative strategies before the customer visit.

* For more photo activities, refer to "*Photo Jolts! Image-based Activities that Increase Clarity, Creativity, and Conversation*" by Glenn Hughes and Sivasailam 'Thiagi' Thiagarajan, available at *Amazon.com*, *BarnesAndNoble.com*, and *PhotoJolts.com*.

ACTIVITY 07
SMART SELECTION

Select a piece of advice and determine which SMART component(s) the advice addresses: Specific, Measureable, Aggressively Attainable, Relevant, or Time-bound?

PURPOSE: Better understand and apply the SMART framework to your goal.

TIME: 5 minutes.

PREPARATION: Download the SMART as Hell Poster from *SMARTasHell.com/blog/SAHAdvice*.

FLOW:

1. *Choose your advice*. Select a piece of advice. Read and reflect on it.
2. *Consider 'Specific"*. Does the advice address specificity? How?
3. *Consider 'Measurable"*. Does the advice address measurability? How?
4. *Consider 'Aggressively Attainable"*. Does the advice address how the goal can be both aggressive and attainable? How?
5. *Consider 'Relevant"*. Does the advice address relevance? How?
6. *Consider 'Time-bound"*. Does the advice address time? How?
7. *Reflect*. How do your findings impact the way you think about your goal? How can the advice change or strengthen your goal?

PLAY SAMPLE

- Pat's goal is to, "Make a sale to a large local company."
- Pat selected Helen Keller's advice, "*Life is either a daring adventure or nothing.*"
- Pat decides that this advice addresses specificity. She believes she needs to articulate exactly how her goal is a daring adventure, or it is nothing.
- Pat thinks that this advice could be about measurability. Is it possible that the only difference between adventure and nothing is scale? Maybe she should set a higher goal?
- Pat is certain that this goal addresses aggressively attainable. She should not set a goal that is merely attainable. She wants to be daring.
- Pat thinks that this advice might address relevance. Is a small sale to a large client as valuable as a large sale to a small client? Maybe she should not focus on large clients?
- Pat decides that this advice does not address time-bound.
- Pat realizes that her goal to make a new sale to a large local company is not adventurous enough.
- Pat will revise her goal to, "Make a $300,000 sale to a large local company."

ACTIVITY 08
DEEP DIVE

Choose one piece of advice and explore it deeply. See how it applies to your situation and your goal.

PURPOSE: Reflect deeply on your goal and your connection to it.

TIME: 20 minutes.

PREPARATION: Download the "*SMART as Hell Advice Reflection Worksheet*" or refer to Table A on page 136.

FLOW:

1. *Download the worksheet.* Download the "*SMART as Hell Advice Reflection Worksheet*" from *SMARTasHell.com/blog/SAHadvice*.
2. *Write your goal.* Write your goal on the worksheet.
3. *Choose your advice.* Select a piece of advice. Read it.
4. *Complete the worksheet.* Take your time and do each of the steps on the worksheet.
5. *Reflect.* What did you learn about your goal? What did you learn about your connection to your goal? What should you change about your goal?
6. *Implement your findings.* Revise your goal or your plan as necessary.

PLAY SAMPLE

- Pat's goal is to, "Make a sale to a large local company."
- Pat selected Helen Keller's advice, "*Life is either a daring adventure or nothing.*"
- Using the worksheet, Pat notes that her confidence is high, but her desire is moderate.
- At each step of the worksheet, the word 'nothing' jolts Pat. She underlines it when she writes the advice. When she reads the advice out loud, the word tastes sour in her mouth.
- When Pat rewrites the advice, she finds herself writing, "My sales career up to now is nothing." This upsets her immensely. She realizes that she expects more from her life than to be an average salesperson.
- Pat decides to dedicate herself fully to her goal for one year. If she is not successful, she vows to consider a career change.

Part Three

Smart as Hell Advice

WEEK 01

MONDAY

A goal is to your life as a map is to your journey.
(Monica Wofford, "Contagious Quotations")

Does your life journey have a map?

TUESDAY

All you have to do is know where you're going.
The answers will come to you of their own accord.
(Earl Nightingale, 'The Strangest Secret')

Where are you going this week?

WEDNESDAY

Success isn't a result of spontaneous combustion.
You must set yourself on fire.
(Attributed to Arnold H. Glasgow)

Does your goal set you on fire?

THURSDAY

Goals are not only absolutely necessary to motivate us.
They are essential to really keep us alive.
(Robert H. Schuller, "Move Ahead with Possibility Thinking")

What goal keeps you alive?

FRIDAY

If you want to make a stand, help others make a stand,
and if you want to reach your goal, help others reach their goal.
(Confucius, "Analects", Trans. Hinton)

Who will you help this week?

SATURDAY / SUNDAY

Remove goals and all you're left with are accidents,
coincidence, luck, and hope.
(Glenn Hughes, SMART as Hell)

Do you feel lucky?

WEEK 02

MONDAY

Measure what is measurable, and make measurable what is not so.

(Attributed to Galileo Galilei)

How will you measure success?

TUESDAY

To play a game you must know the rules,
the stakes, and the quitting time.

(Chinese Proverb)

Are you ready to play your game?

WEDNESDAY

If one casts a small net, one cannot catch big fish.

(Proverb)

Is your goal big enough to catch big fish?

THURSDAY

It is not enough to be industrious; so are the ants.
The question is: What are you industrious about?
(Henry David Thoreau, walden.org)
So, what are you busy about?

FRIDAY

The time is always right to do what's right.
(Martin Luther King, oberlin.edu)
What's the right thing for you to do today?

SATURDAY / SUNDAY

All things are created twice. There's a mental or first creation,
and a physical or second creation, to all things.
(Stephen R. Covey, "The 7 Habits of Highly Effective People")
Does your goal help you mentally create your 'thing'?

WEEK 03

MONDAY

The only reason for time is so that everything doesn't happen at once. (Attributed to Albert Einstein)

Do all of your deadlines happen at once?

TUESDAY

Not everything that counts can be counted. Not everything that can be counted counts. (Attributed to Albert Einstein)

Are you doing the things that count?

WEDNESDAY

Whoever undertakes to set himself up as a judge of Truth and Knowledge is shipwrecked by the laughter of the gods. (Albert Einstein, "The Ultimate Quotable Einstein")

Are you ready to stop judging and start learning?

THURSDAY

If you want to live a happy life,
tie it to a goal, not to people or objects.
(Albert Einstein, "The Ultimate Quotable Einstein")

What goal is your life tied to?

FRIDAY

It's not that I'm so smart, it's just that I stay with problems longer.
(Attributed to Albert Einstein)

Will you stay with your goal long enough to achieve it?

SATURDAY / SUNDAY

The levels of intelligence are
"Smart, intelligent, brilliant, genius, simple."
(Attributed to Albert Einstein)

Can you simplify your challenge?

WEEK 04

MONDAY

Everything is vague to a degree you do not realize till you have tried to make it precise.
(Bertrand Russell, "The Philosophy of Logical Atomism")

Is your goal vague or precise?

TUESDAY

What gets measured gets done.
(Unknown)

Can you measure progress against your goal?

WEDNESDAY

Life is either a daring adventure or nothing.
(Helen Keller, "Let Us Have Faith")

What is your daring adventure?

THURSDAY

Almost any activity can be made engaging with reasonably challenging goals and frequent feedback. (Joseph Grenny et al., "Influencer")

What boring activity can you make engaging?

FRIDAY

There is surely nothing quite so useless as doing with great efficiency what should not be done at all. (Peter Drucker, 'Drucker on Managerial Change', Harvard Business Review)

What useless task can you stop doing brilliantly?

SATURDAY / SUNDAY

A time frame that is too long will remove any sense of urgency. (Attributed to Beverly Kaye)

Can you shorten the timeframe of your goal?

WEEK 05

MONDAY

To be able to experience flow, one must have clear goals to strive for.

(Mihaly Csikszentmihalyi, "Finding Flow")

Do you have clear goals?

TUESDAY

They [goals] focus psychic energy, establish priorities
and thus create order in consciousness.
(Mihaly Csikszentmihalyi, "Finding Flow")

Do you have order in your consciousness?

WEDNESDAY

Without them [goals], mental processes become random
and feelings tend to deteriorate rapidly.
(Mihaly Csikszentmihalyi, "Finding Flow")

Do you ever feel like your mental processes are random?

THURSDAY

A man's reach should exceed his grasp.

(Mihaly Csikszentmihalyi, "Good Business")

Does your goal exceed your grasp?

FRIDAY

Eventually it is the goals that we pursue that will shape and determine the kind of self that we are to become.

(Mihaly Csikszentmihalyi, "Finding Flow")

Based on your goal, who will you become?

SATURDAY / SUNDAY

And more than anything else, the self represents the hierarchy of goals that we have built up, bit by bit, over the years.

(Mihaly Csikszentmihalyi, "Flow")

What goals from the past created who you are today?

WEEK 06

MONDAY

Never stand in front of a judge or behind a donkey.
(Indian proverb, "Facts on File Dictionary of Proverbs")

Who will judge the success of your goal?

TUESDAY

Judging is a lonely job in which a man is, as near as may be, an island entire. (Abe Fortas, 'Yale Law Journal')

Is your judge qualified for the burden of judging you?

WEDNESDAY

When you judge another, you do not define them, you define yourself.
(Attributed to Wayne Dyer)

What bias does your judge have?

THURSDAY

Criticism may not be agreeable, but it is necessary. It fulfills the same function as pain in the human body. It calls attention to an unhealthy state of things. (Winston Churchill, newstatesman.com)

Are you ready to be criticized?

FRIDAY

To judge between good or bad, between successful and unsuccessful would take the eye of god. (Attributed to Anton Chekhov)

Does your goal force someone to play god?

SATURDAY / SUNDAY

Repeatedly it was found that people who were assigned difficult goals performed better than those who were assigned moderately difficult goals. (Locke & Latham, "Goal Setting")

Is your goal difficult enough?

WEEK 07

MONDAY

I keep six honest serving men (they taught me all I knew); their names are what and why and when, and how and where and who.
(Rudyard Kipling, "Just So Stories")

Does your goal serve all six honest men?

TUESDAY

Remember, a goal without a number is just a slogan.
(Canfield et al., "The Power of Focus")

Does your goal have a number?

WEDNESDAY

Big goals get big results.
No goals gets no results or somebody else's results.
(Mark Victor Hansen, "Wake Up... Live the Life You Love")

Is your goal big?

THURSDAY

*Doing what should not be done will bring ruin,
and not doing what should be done will also bring ruin.
(Tiruvalluvar, "Tirukural", Trans. Subramuniyaswami)*

Are you doing what should be done?

FRIDAY

*As if you could kill time without injuring eternity!
(Henry David Thoreau, "Walden")*

Are you just killing time?

SATURDAY / SUNDAY

*If you are working for an organization,
expedition goal setting is not an entirely democratic process.
("Leadership the Outward Bound Way")*

Is too much input compromising your goal?

WEEK 08

MONDAY

Man is a goal-seeking animal. His life only has meaning if he is reaching out and striving for his goals.

(Attributed to Aristotle)

Are you reaching out and striving for meaningful goals?

TUESDAY

Better to light a candle than to curse the darkness.

(Proverb)

Are you lighting a candle or cursing the darkness?

WEDNESDAY

By losing your goal, you have lost your way.

(Attributed to both Friedrich Nietzsche and Kahlil Gibran)

Have you lost your way?

THURSDAY

*How wonderful it is that no one has to wait,
but can start right now to gradually change the world.
(Anne Frank, "Tales from the Secret Annex")*

How does your goal improve the world?

FRIDAY

*If the single man plant himself indomitably on his instincts,
and there abide, the huge world will come round to him.
(Ralph Waldo Emerson,
"Essays and Poems by Ralph Waldo Emerson")*

Are you following your instincts?

SATURDAY / SUNDAY

*Values mediate the path of action. Goals release the energy.
(Kouzes & Posner, "The Leadership Challenge")*

Are your goals in alignment with your values?

WEEK 09

MONDAY

I went to a general store but they wouldn't let me buy anything specific. (Attributed to Stephen Wright)

Is your goal general or specific?

TUESDAY

It is never freedom till you find something you really positively want to be. (D. H. Lawrence, "Studies in Classic American Literature, Volume 2")

What do you really want to be?

WEDNESDAY

He who has a Why to live for can bear almost any How. (Attributed to Friedrich Nietzsche)

Is your 'why' important enough to bear any 'how'?

THURSDAY

If not now then when?

(Attributed to Rabbi Hillel)

What can you do today?

FRIDAY

A BHAG (Big Hairy Audacious Goal) serves as a unifying point of effort, galvanizing people and creating team spirit as people strive toward a finish line. (Jim Collins, "Good to Great")

Is your goal a BHAG?

SATURDAY / SUNDAY

Half of being smart is knowing what you are dumb about.

(Attributed to Solomon Short)

Are you getting help where you need it?

Week 10

MONDAY

Before accepting death you should know what your objective is and achieve your goal before your last breath.
(Yamamoto Tsunetomo, "The Hagakure", Trans. D.E. Tarver)

Do you have a samurai's commitment to your goal?

TUESDAY

An unworried expression is one sign that a person is focused on accomplishing a major goal with his entire soul.
(Yamamoto Tsunetomo, "The Hagakure", Trans. D.E. Tarver)

What's your expression?

WEDNESDAY

A warrior should always set his mind on the highest goals in all that he does.
(Yamamoto Tsunetomo, "The Hagakure", Trans. D.E. Tarver)

Is this goal your highest goal?

THURSDAY

A warrior who is ready to go to any length to achieve his goal cannot be stopped by even a multitude of samurai.
(Yamamoto Tsunetomo, "The Hagakure", Trans. D.E. Tarver)

What lengths are you ready to go to for your goal?

FRIDAY

Make your decision, resolve your heart, calm your spirit, refresh your mind, and then break through every barrier until you reach your goal.
(Yamamoto Tsunetomo, "The Hagakure", Trans. D.E. Tarver)

Are you resolved, calm, and refreshed?

SATURDAY / SUNDAY

If you don't have an exit strategy, don't count on a smooth exit.
(Glenn Hughes, SMART as Hell)

Does your goal give you an exit strategy?

WEEK 11

MONDAY

The difference between the almost right word and the right word is really a large matter – 'tis the difference between the lightning bug and the lightning. (Mark Twain, "The Art of Authorship")

Are you the lightning bug? or the lightning?

TUESDAY

The trouble with measurement is its seeming simplicity.
(Unknown)

Are you assuming you can measure your goal accurately?

WEDNESDAY

When walking, walk. When eating, eat.
(Zen maxim)

Are you focused? or distracted?

THURSDAY

A wealth of research - at least 200 studies - proves that challenging employees to meet goals motivates higher performance. (Wagner & Harter, "12, The Elements of Great Managing")

Will your goal motivate higher performance?

FRIDAY

*You may delay, but time will not.
(Benjamin Franklin, "Poor Richard's Almanack")*

Are you taking action on your goal?

SATURDAY / SUNDAY

One out of seven has been so obsessed with achieving a goal that at one point in their lives they broke the law or did something unethical. (Stephen Shapiro, "Goal Free Living")

Could you succumb to goal obsession?

WEEK 12

MONDAY

More men fail through lack of purpose than lack of talent.

(Attributed to Billy Sunday)

Have you lacked purpose in your life?

TUESDAY

To forget one's purpose is the commonest form of stupidity.

(Attributed to Friedrich Nietzsche)

Do you know your purpose now?

WEDNESDAY

The secret of success is constancy to purpose.

(Attributed to Benjamin Disraeli)

Are you constant to your purpose?

THURSDAY

Goals are a way of aligning our actions to our purpose.
(Niemela & Lewis, "Leading High Impact Teams")

Does your goal align to your purpose?

FRIDAY

It may be that your whole purpose in life is simply to serve as a warning to others. (Unknown)

Will your life be more than a cautionary tale?

SATURDAY / SUNDAY

Be not simply good; be good for something.
(Henry David Thoreau, 'The Eagle and the Serpent')

What will you be good for?

WEEK 13

MONDAY

Devote your entire will power to mastering one thing at a time; do not scatter your energies.

(Paramahansa Yogananada, "The Law of Success")

Do your goals focus your energies? or scatter them?

TUESDAY

Measure progress. Goals only work if you measure progress.

(Guy Kawasaki, "Art of the Start")

How often are you measuring progress?

WEDNESDAY

Never leave that till tomorrow which you can do today.

(Benjamin Franklin, "Poor Richard's Almanack")

What will you do today to further your goal?

THURSDAY

Focus your mind on your goal, constantly strive to attain perfection, and do not allow yourself to be sidetracked.
(Miyamoto Musashi, "The Book of Five Rings", Trans. Kaufmann)

How will you avoid being sidetracked?

FRIDAY

Ideally, each employee should set enrichment goals.
(Kaye & Jordan-Evans, "Love 'Em or Lose 'Em")

Does your goal enrich you?

SATURDAY / SUNDAY

A well-written goal is not a substitute for ideas or talent.
(Glenn Hughes, SMART as Hell)

Does your goal support great ideas and strong talent?

Week 14

MONDAY

Too many people make decisions based on outcomes rather than process. (Paul DePodesta, "Moneyball" by Michael Lewis)

Does your goal focus on process? or on outcomes?

TUESDAY

He'll never go anywhere because he doesn't look like a big league ballplayer. ("Moneyball" by Michael Lewis)

Does your goal focus on the superficial?

WEDNESDAY

Of all the positive events that influence inner work life, the single most powerful is progress in meaningful work. (Teresa Amabile, "The Progress Principle")

Can you track the progress of your work?

THURSDAY

Baseball data conflated luck and skill and simply ignored a lot of what happened during a baseball game.
(Michael Lewis, "Moneyball")

Does your goal confuse luck with skill?

FRIDAY

Many of the players drafted or acquired by the Oakland A's had been the victims of an unthinking prejudice rooted in baseball's traditions. (Michael Lewis, "Moneyball")

Is your goal based on outdated standards?

SATURDAY / SUNDAY

... a person should have at least three, and preferably many more, possible ways to reach his goal before he plunges. (Robert H. Schuller, "Move Ahead with Possibility Thinking")

How many possible ways can you reach your goal?

Week 15

MONDAY

You cannot make it as a wandering generality.
You must become a meaningful specific.
(Zig Ziglar, "Pick Four")

Are you a 'meaningful specific'?

TUESDAY

To let fly an arrow where there is no enemy.
("Japanese Proverbs")

Are you wasting arrows?

WEDNESDAY

[Have a] Soaring / Bold / Noble Purpose.
(Tom Peters, "The Little Big Things")

Is your goal 'soaring', 'bold', and 'noble'?

THURSDAY

*Measure everything of significance. I swear this is true.
Anything that is measured and watched, improves.
(Bob Parsons, from "Inspire!" by Jim Champy)*

Are you watching what you measure?

FRIDAY

*I wasted time, and now doth time waste me.
(Shakespeare, "Richard II")*

Is time wasting you?

SATURDAY / SUNDAY

*The trees of difficulty and ease share
the same root system - vagueness.
(Glenn Hughes, SMART as Hell)*

Does vagueness undermine your goal?

WEEK 16

MONDAY

You ever try to go a day without judgment?
(Attributed to Max Cannon)

Do your goals free you from judgment?

TUESDAY

The average man's judgment is so poor; he runs a risk every time he uses it. (Attributed to Edgar Watson Howe)

Does your goal reduce the risk inherent in judgment?

WEDNESDAY

But I am, as I am; whether hideous, or handsome, depends upon who is made judge.
(Herman Melville, "Mardi and a Voyage Thither")

Does your goal minimize bias?

THURSDAY

Never trust the artist. Trust the tale. (D. H. Lawrence, "Studies in Classic American Literature, Volume 2")

Will the achievement of your goal tell your tale honestly?

FRIDAY

It may be you fear more to deliver judgment upon me than I fear judgment. (Giordano Bruno, from "Educating as Art")

Does your goal free others from the burden of judgment?

SATURDAY / SUNDAY

Objectives are not fate; they are directions.
They are not commands; they are commitments.
(Peter Drucker, "The Essential Drucker")

Are you committed to the direction of your goal?

WEEK 17

MONDAY

All my life, I always wanted to be somebody. But I see now I should have been more specific. (Jane Wagner, "The Search for Signs of Intelligent Life in the Universe")

Are you specific about what you want to be?

TUESDAY

Rubrics help improve performance as they reduce uncertainty and ambiguity. (Fred C. Bolton, 'Rubrics and Adult Learners')

Would your goal benefit from using a rubric?

WEDNESDAY

Always do more than is required of you. (George S. Patton, from "Patton: A Genius for War" by Carlo D'Este)

Are you planning to exceed expectations?

THURSDAY

A goal without a deadline is only a wish.
A dream with a deadline becomes a goal.
("Best Loved Chinese Proverbs" by Lau & Lau)
Do you have a firm deadline for your goal?

FRIDAY

Focus on eliminating anything that doesn't serve the fulfillment of your goals. (Michael J. Gelb, "Innovate Like Edison")
What will you stop doing today?

SATURDAY / SUNDAY

Intelligence, then, is the ability to attain goals in the face of obstacles by means of decisions based on natural rules. (Stephen Pinker, "How the Mind Works")
Are you ready to overcome the obstacles to your goal?

WEEK 18

MONDAY

The things that get rewarded get done. (Michael LeBoef, "The Greatest Management Principle in the World")

What are you rewarded for?

TUESDAY

You get what you reward. Be clear about what you want to get and systematically reward it. (Attributed to Bob Nelson)

Are your rewards tied to your goal?

WEDNESDAY

Reward the achievers. (Guy Kawasaki, "Reality Check")

Are <u>only</u> the achievers rewarded?

THURSDAY

*There is nothing man will not attempt
when great enterprises hold out the promise of great rewards.
(Titus Livius, "The Routledge Dictionary of Latin Quotations")*

Are there great rewards for achieving your goal?

FRIDAY

*People who create 20% of the results will begin believing
they deserve 80% of the rewards.
(Attributed to Pat Riley)*

Does your goal clarify who deserves rewards?

SATURDAY / SUNDAY

*Believe me, the reward is not so great without the struggle.
(Wilma Rudolph, chicagotribune.com)*

Does your goal require a struggle?

Week 19

MONDAY

Competition is the whetstone of talent. (Unknown)

Who (or what) is your competition?

TUESDAY

In business, the competition will bite you if you keep running, if you stand still, they will swallow you.
(Attributed to William Kundsen)

Will your goal keep you ahead of your competition?

WEDNESDAY

A competitive world offers two possibilities. You can lose. Or, if you want to win, you can change.
(Unknown)

What changes will you make today?

THURSDAY

*Of all human powers operating on the affairs of mankind,
none is greater than that of competition.
(Henry Clay, from "Plantation Capitalism" by Ray Mills Antley)*

Will your goal generate competition?

FRIDAY

*Competition provides spice in life as well as in sports; it's only when
the spice becomes the entire diet that the player gets sick.
(George Leonard, "Mastery")*

Does your goal generate too much competition?

SATURDAY / SUNDAY

*Competition brings out the best in products
and the worst in people. (Attributed to David Sarnoff)*

Will your goal bring out the worst in you and others?

Week 20

MONDAY

Create goals that give a sense of real, not false, urgency.
(Niemela & Lewis, "Leading High Impact Teams")
Do you feel real urgency towards your goal?

TUESDAY

How can you distinguish a shortcut from a distraction
if you don't know what the goal is?
(Marcus Buckingham, "The One Thing You Need to Know")
Does your goal help you eliminate distractions?

WEDNESDAY

If you run after two hares, you will catch neither.
(Proverb)
Is your goal singular in purpose?

THURSDAY

I do urge you to pay the closest attention to the ART of Milestoning. Become a milestone activist. Use milestoning as a matter of routine.
(Tom Peters, "The Little Big Things")

Is your goal supported by frequent milestones?

FRIDAY

Find performance indicators that will lead you toward the goal.
(Rajesh Setty, "Beyond Code")

Do you have useful performance indicators?

SATURDAY / SUNDAY

Happiness cannot be pursued; it must ensue.
One must have a reason to "be happy".
(Viktor Frankl, "Man's Search for Meaning")

What is the reason for your goal?

WEEK 21

MONDAY

The main thing is to keep the main thing the main thing. (Stephen R. Covey, "First Things First")

Is your goal the main thing?

TUESDAY

The closer people get to completing a goal, the more effort they exert to achieve that goal. (Robert Cialdini, "Yes!")

Does progress towards your goal inspire more effort?

WEDNESDAY

One way to keep momentum going is to have constantly greater goals. (Michael Korda, "Success!")

Is your current goal greater than your last goal?

THURSDAY

Design a simple visibility system that will make it apparent whether you're progressing toward your goal.
(Edward Muzio, "Make Work Great")

Can you tell when you're getting closer to your goal?

FRIDAY

You are never too old to set another goal or to dream a new dream.
(Unknown)

What's your new dream?

SATURDAY / SUNDAY

The only sure way to create a successful presentation is to begin with a goal in mind. (Jerry Weisman, "Presenting to Win")

Do your presentations start with a goal in mind?

WEEK 22

MONDAY

God is in the details. (Unknown)

Is your goal detailed enough for everyone to understand?

TUESDAY

God is in the details… and so is your reward.
(Glenn Hughes, SMART as Hell)

Will the details prove that you earned your reward?

WEDNESDAY

I am not interested in the past. I am interested in the future, for that is where I expect to spend the rest of my life.
(Attributed to Charles F. Kettering)

Is your goal leading you into the future?

THURSDAY

*They just need some gutsy, challenging goals to help them get there.
(Mark Murphy, "Hundred Percenters")*

Is your goal gutsy?

FRIDAY

*We achieve our goals by focusing on what we want,
not on what we don't want.
(Brian Biro, "Beyond Success")*

Are you too focused on what you <u>don't</u> want?

SATURDAY / SUNDAY

There has been progress, but starting from a regrettably low baseline. (Andy Hayman, theguardian.com)

Is your progress enough to make a difference?

WEEK 23

MONDAY

*A man without a purpose is like a ship without a rudder –
a waif, a nothing, a no man.*
(Attributed to Thomas Carlyle)

Do you have a purpose?

TUESDAY

Success demands singleness of purpose.
(Vince Lombardi, "Run to Daylight")

Are you focused on your purpose?

WEDNESDAY

Definiteness of purpose is the starting point of all achievement.
(Hill & Stone, "Success Through a Positive Mental Attitude")

Are you definite about your purpose?

THURSDAY

Edison's purpose was clear: "Bringing out the secrets of nature and applying them for the happiness of man".
(Michael J. Gelb, "Innovate Like Edison")

Is your purpose as clear as Edison's?

FRIDAY

The first thing to do in life is to do with purpose what one purposes.
(Attributed to Pablo Casals)

Are you pursuing your purpose <u>with</u> purpose?

SATURDAY / SUNDAY

Many managers do, of course, set and define goals; they trip up, however, because they overoperationalize the jobs.
(Coffman & Gonzalez-Molina, "Follow This Path")

Are your goals overoperationalized?

WEEK 24

MONDAY

Goals regulate performance far better when feedback is present than when it is absent. (Locke & Latham, "New Developments in Goal Setting and Task Performance")

What is your feedback system?

TUESDAY

Feedback is the breakfast of champions. (Ken Blanchard, "The New One Minute Manager")

Did you get your feedback today?

WEDNESDAY

Champions know that success is inevitable; that there is no such thing as failure, only feedback. (Attributed to Michael J. Gelb)

How can you turn a recent setback into feedback?

THURSDAY

We judge ourselves by what we feel capable of doing, while others judge us by what we have already done. (Henry Wadsworth Longfellow, "Kavanaugh")

Are you judging your potential? or your performance?

FRIDAY

I mistrust the judgment of every man in a case in which his own wishes are concerned. (The Duke of Wellington, from "Characteristics of the Duke of Wellington" by The Earl De Grey)

Can you trust that your evaluators are not tainted?

SATURDAY / SUNDAY

All speech without action appears vain and idle. (Demosthenes, from "Olympiac", Trans. Kennedy)

Are you backing your goal with action?

WEEK 25

MONDAY

If one does not know to which port one is sailing, no wind is favorable. (Lucius Annaeus Seneca, "Moral Letters to Lucilius")

Are you doing a lot, but going nowhere?

🍂

TUESDAY

If you can't chart it, don't start it.
(Glenn Hughes, SMART as Hell)

Can you track your goal on a chart?

🍂

WEDNESDAY

If you're really serious about accomplishing your goal, plot your progress on a chart.
(Robert F. Mager, "Goal Analysis")

Are you plotting your progress?

THURSDAY

*Encourage people to choose battles big enough to matter
but small enough to win. (Michael Leboeuf,
"The Greatest Management Principle in the World")*

Did you choose the right battle?

FRIDAY

*People should decide what success means for them,
and not be distracted by accepting others' definitions of success.
(Attributed to Tony Levin)*

Who is defining your success?

SATURDAY / SUNDAY

*Get a challenge to push you,
get a goal to push you, get a deadline to push you.
(Richard St. John, "Stupid, Unlucky, Ugly, and Rich")*

What's pushing you?

WEEK 26

MONDAY

Adventure is just bad planning.
(Attributed to Roald Amudsen)

Do you have a good plan?

TUESDAY

Victorious warriors win first then go to war.
(Zhang Yu, from "The Art of War", Trans. Cleary)

Have you won before you started?

WEDNESDAY

Plans are nothing. Planning is everything.
(Dwight D. Eisenhower, presidency.ucsb.edu)

Did you engage in a thorough planning process?

THURSDAY

When it is obvious that the goals cannot be reached, don't adjust the goals, adjust the action plans. (Attributed to Confucius)

Can you hold to your goal, while adjusting your plan?

FRIDAY

Make your years plans in spring and your days plans in the morning. ("ABC Dictionary of Chinese Proverbs")

Do you make fresh daily plans?

SATURDAY / SUNDAY

Never tell people how to do things. Tell them what to do and they will surprise you with their ingenuity. (George S. Patton, "War As I Knew It")

Do you allow others to create their own plans?

WEEK 27

MONDAY

The tool kit of a problem-solving kid includes identifying the root cause of a problem and setting specific goals. (Ken Watanabe, "Problem Solving 101")

Do you know the root cause of your problem?

TUESDAY

The man who says he is willing to meet you halfway is usually a poor judge of distance. (Attributed to Laurence J. Peter)

Do all parties agree on the measurements?

WEDNESDAY

If you look up there are no limits. ("Japanese Proverbs and Sayings")

Are you held back by your perceived limits?

THURSDAY

Many times as I work with organizations, I find people whose goals are totally different from the goals of the enterprise. (Steven R. Covey, "The 7 Habits of Highly Effective People")

Are your goals aligned with those around you?

FRIDAY

Deadlines are absolutely necessary in a creative environment. (Richard St. John, "Stupid, Ugly, Unlucky, and Rich")

What creative projects in your life lack deadlines?

SATURDAY / SUNDAY

Silence is sometimes the severest criticism. ("A Dictionary of American Proverbs")

Do you skip feedback, thinking 'no news is good news'?

WEEK 28

MONDAY

Average performers are goal driven; peak performers are mission driven. (Blanchard & Woodring, "Empowerment")

Is your goal connected to a higher mission?

TUESDAY

When people lose Mojo, the cause can often be traced to a rootless sense of mission. They lack clear goals. They don't target opportunities. (Marshall Goldsmith, "Mojo")

Are you targeting your opportunities?

WEDNESDAY

Roles and goals give structure and organized direction to your personal mission. (Steven R. Covey, "The 7 Habits of Highly Effective People")

Do you know your role in achieving this goal?

THURSDAY

Vision without action is a daydream.

Action without vision is a nightmare. (Japanese Proverb)

Are you acting in alignment with a vision?

FRIDAY

Oh, the vision thing... (George H. W. Bush, from "The Rhetorical Presidency of George H. W. Bush" by Martin Medhurst)

Be honest, are you still skeptical about the value of vision?

SATURDAY / SUNDAY

In more than one thousand studies conducted by researchers across the globe, they've found out that goals that spell out exactly what needs to be accomplished and that set the bar for achievement high, result in far superior performance than goals that are vague or that set the bar too low.

(Heidi Grant Halverson, "Succeed")

Is your goal specific and aggressive?

WEEK 29

MONDAY

Time is what we want most but what, alas! we use worst.

(William Penn, "Some Fruits of Solitude")

How are you using your time?

TUESDAY

One who straddles two boats is likely to fall into water.

(Proverb)

What other goal is distracting you from this goal?

WEDNESDAY

Goals without feedback and feedback without goals have little effect on motivation.

(Kouzes & Posner, "Encouraging the Heart")

Are you giving feedback that's unrelated to goals?

THURSDAY

Are you doing things right? Or are you doing the right things?
(Unknown)

Can you tell what is the right thing to do?

FRIDAY

Conditions of learning: the learners have a sense of progress towards their goals. (Malcolm Knowles, "The Adult Learner")

Can you tell if you're learning?

SATURDAY / SUNDAY

People withhold their best efforts when they see little or no relationship between what they do and how they are rewarded.
(Michael Leboeuf,
"The Greatest Management Principle in the World")

Is your goal tied to rewards?

WEEK 30

MONDAY

You must be able to set accurate performance expectations.
(Marcus Buckingham, "First Break All the Rules")

Do you have accurate performance expectations?

TUESDAY

A critic is a bundle of biases held loosely together by a sense of taste.
(Whitney Balliett, "The Oxford Dictionary of Quotations")

What biases do your critics possess?

WEDNESDAY

Is this goal fundamentally wimpy?
(Mark Murphy, leadershipnow.com)

Is it?

THURSDAY

We get too soon old and too late smart. (Unknown)

How long will you wait make your goal SMART as Hell?

❞

FRIDAY

When a goal matters enough to a person, that person will find a way to accomplish what at first seemed impossible. (Attributed to Nido Qubein)

Does your goal matter to you?

❞

SATURDAY / SUNDAY

Good BHAGs [Big Hairy Audacious Goals] flow from understanding. Bad BHAGs flow from bravado. (Jim Collins, "Good to Great")

Was your goal set with understanding? or bravado?

WEEK 31

MONDAY

A goal properly set is halfway reached.
(Attributed to Abraham Lincoln)

Is your goal properly set?

TUESDAY

Only the disciplined are free.
(James Cash Penney, 'The Rotarian')

Are you disciplined in the pursuit of your goal?

WEDNESDAY

There are many roads to success, but the right road for any inventor begins with finding an opportunity and setting a goal.
(Stanley Mason, "Inventing Small Products")

What's your opportunity?

THURSDAY

When your work speaks for itself, don't interrupt.

(Attributed to Henry J. Kaiser)

Does your work speak for itself?

FRIDAY

I often say that when you can measure what you are speaking about, and express it in numbers, you know something about it.

(Lord Kelvin, 'Electrical Units of Measurement')

Can you express your work in numbers?

SATURDAY / SUNDAY

Nobody should be judge in his own cause.

("Facts on File Dictionary of Proverbs")

Can you get a neutral assessment of your performance?

WEEK 32

MONDAY

Don't overextend yourself by attempting too much change with too many goals. (Hughes & Beatty, "Becoming a Strategic Leader")

Do you have too many goals?

TUESDAY

It is a terrible feeling to regret not going after your biggest, most meaningful goals. (Larina Kase, "The Confident Leader")

What do you regret not going after?

WEDNESDAY

*There is no such thing as measurement absolute, there is only measurement relative.
(Jeanette Winterson, "Gut Symmetries")*

Do you have context to your measurements?

THURSDAY

Let your stars set the bars.

(Glenn Hughes, SMART as Hell)

Would your goal challenge a star performer?

FRIDAY

Goals are dreams with deadlines.

(Unknown)

Can you put a deadline on one of your dreams?

SATURDAY / SUNDAY

Unless commitment is made,
there are only promises and hopes... but no plans.

(Peter Drucker, "The Daily Drucker")

Are you committed to this goal?

WEEK 33

MONDAY

*A person who does not have a clear goal
is used by someone who does.
(Blanchard & Woodring, "Empowerment")*

Are you spending your energies on someone else's goal?

TUESDAY

*Goals determine what you're going to be.
(Julius Erving, from "Doc" by Vincent Mallozzi)*

Based on your goal, what are you going to be?

WEDNESDAY

*A specification that will not fit on one page of 8.5x11
inch paper cannot be understood. (Attributed to Mark Ardis)*

Is your goal and plan succinct?

THURSDAY

The soul which has no fixed goal loses itself; for as they say, to be everywhere is to be nowhere. (Michel de Montaigne, from "The Complete Essays of Montaigne", Trans. Frame)

Is your soul lost?

FRIDAY

Make your work to be in keeping with your purpose. (Attributed to Leonardo da Vinci)

Is your work aligned with your purpose?

SATURDAY / SUNDAY

I love deadlines. I like the whooshing sound they make as they fly by. (Attributed to Douglas Adams)

Can you hear your deadlines whooshing by?

WEEK 34

MONDAY

Being crystal clear on your goal is the first and crucial step in successful innovation. (David Nichols, "Return On Ideas")

Are you crystal clear on your goal?

TUESDAY

The reward for conformity was that everyone liked you but yourself. (Rita Mae Brown, "Venus Envy")

Are you letting others determine your goals?

WEDNESDAY

Postpone, or at least de-emphasize, touchy-feely goals. (Guy Kawasaki, "Reality Check")

You didn't write a 'feel-good' goal, did you?

THURSDAY

If you cannot weigh, measure, number your results, however you may be convinced yourself, you must not hope to convince others, or claim the position of an investigator; you are merely a guesser, a propounder of hypotheses. (Frederick Gard Fleay, 'On Metrical Tests as Applied to Dramatic Poetry')

Are you merely a guesser of your results?

FRIDAY

Success is the sole earthly judge of right and wrong. (Attributed to Adolf Hitler)

Do you believe success is the sole judge of your goal?

SATURDAY / SUNDAY

I learned you can't trust the judgment of good friends. (Carl Sandburg, "Ever the Winds of Chance")

Who do you trust to judge your work?

WEEK 35

MONDAY

In whatever position you find yourself determine first your objective.
(Attributed to Marshall Ferdinand Foch)

Have you determined your objective?

TUESDAY

Objectives must make possible concentration of resources and efforts. They must, therefore, be selective rather than encompass everything.
(Peter Drucker, "The Essential Drucker")

Are your resources concentrated? or scattered?

WEDNESDAY

It doesn't matter where you live. If you have a goal in mind, you can turn any venue or destination into a valuable field trip.
(Twyla Tharp, "The Creative Habit")

What's your next valuable field trip?

THURSDAY

The only man who behaves sensibly is my tailor; he takes my measurements anew every time he sees me, while all the rest go on with their old measurements and expect me to fit them.
(George Bernard Shaw, "Man and Superman")

Do your old goals still fit you?

FRIDAY

If you get all the facts, your judgment can be right; if you don't get all the facts, it can't be right.
(Bernard Baruch, from "Great Jewish Quotations")

Do you have all the facts?

SATURDAY / SUNDAY

Against criticism a man can neither protest nor defend himself; he must act in spite of it, and then it will gradually yield to him.
(Johann Wolfgang von Goethe, "Maxims and Reflections")

Is criticism stopping you from taking action? Why?

WEEK 36

MONDAY

The naked eye was an inadequate tool for learning what you needed to know to evaluate baseball players and baseball games. (Michael Lewis, "Moneyball")

Is your measurement better than a 'naked eye' assessment?

TUESDAY

Once the goal has been reached, a natural, subconscious letdown often occurs. (Brian Biro, "Beyond Success")

How can you combat a letdown?

WEDNESDAY

If professional baseball players could be over- or under-valued, who couldn't? (Michael Lewis, "Moneyball")

Do others over- or under-value you?

THURSDAY

There was also a tendency to be overly influenced by a guy's most recent performance. What he did last was not necessarily what he would do next. (Michael Lewis, "Moneyball")

Are you overly influenced by recent performance?

FRIDAY

There are two tragedies in life. One is to lose your heart's desire. The other is to gain it. (George Bernard Shaw, "Man and Superman")

Is the tragedy missing your goal? or achieving it?

SATURDAY / SUNDAY

What begins as a failure of the imagination ends as a market inefficiency: when you rule out an entire class of people from doing a job simply by their appearance, you are less likely to find the best person for the job. (Michael Lewis, "Moneyball")

Does your goal measure and identify the 'best'?

Week 37

MONDAY

You've got to be very careful if you don't know where you are going, because you might not get there.

(Yogi Berra, "What Time Is It? You Mean Now?")

Will your goal get you 'there'?

TUESDAY

Constant dripping wears away a stone.

("Facts on File Dictionary of Proverbs")

What will you do today to wear away at your goal?

WEDNESDAY

You come most carefully upon your hour.

(Shakespeare, "Hamlet")

When is your hour?

THURSDAY

*I say, follow your bliss and don't be afraid,
and doors will open where didn't know they were going to be.
(Joseph Campbell, "The Power of Myth")*

Does this goal help you follow your bliss?

FRIDAY

*With competition everyone has to try harder.
(Attributed to Harold H. Greene)*

Are you working harder than your competition?

SATURDAY / SUNDAY

*What's being rewarded?
(Michael LeBoeuf, "The Greatest Management Principle")*

Are the current rewards reinforcing your goal?

WEEK 38

MONDAY

You form a team with a goal and when the goal is over, the team dissolves. And then, you form a new team with a new goal until that's over. (Helen Fisher, tompeters.com)

Are you using the right team on your new goal?

TUESDAY

Getting individuals to mesh their goals with team goals is your goal. (John Wooden, "The Essential Wooden")

Do the individual and team goals mesh?

WEDNESDAY

The incredibly challenging deadline and shared goal had helped create a spirited 'hot group'. (Tom Kelly, "The Art of Innovation")

Do you have a 'hot group' working on your goal?

THURSDAY

In cross-functional groups, people may not see eye to eye on things, particularly if they have conflicting goals. (Hughes & Beatty, "Becoming a Strategic Leader")

Do your goals conflict with the goals of others?

FRIDAY

The best teamwork comes from men who are working independently toward one goal in unison. (Attributed to James Cash Penney)

Is your team working in unison?

SATURDAY / SUNDAY

Ask your team members to identify at least three personal dreams and connect those with corporate goals. (Terry Barber, "The Inspiration Factor")

Does your team connect their dreams with your goals?

WEEK 39

MONDAY

If you aim at nothing, you'll hit it every time.

(Unknown)

Are you aiming at nothing?

TUESDAY

Most military histories of the Vietnam War agree on the reason for the defeat: the military had no unified strategic doctrine, no clear definition of victory. (Mark Fuller, fastcompany.com)

How do you define victory?

WEDNESDAY

You will never get any more out of life than you expect. Every man today is the result of his thoughts of yesterday.

(Bruce Lee, "Striking Thoughts")

What do you expect of yourself?

THURSDAY

37% of the 400 richest Americans are unhappy.

(Joshua Piven, "As Luck Would Have It")

Will the pursuit of your goal bring happiness?

FRIDAY

Every step that we take […] should be done in a sacred manner; each step should be as a prayer.

(Plains Indian Song, "Mystic Warriors of the Plains")

Do you take each step of your goal seriously?

SATURDAY / SUNDAY

Lorne told me, "We don't go on the air because the show's ready; we go on because it's eleven-thirty." (Darrell Hammond, from "Live From New York" by Miller & Shales)

Does your deadline increase the activity on your goal?

WEEK 40

MONDAY

Follow effective action with quiet reflection.

(Attributed to Peter Drucker)

Do you take time to reflect on your results?

TUESDAY

I do not believe in a fate that falls on men however they act;
but I do believe in a fate that falls on them unless they act.

(G. K. Chesterton, "Generally Speaking")

Are you leaving your fate to fate?

WEDNESDAY

Do not waste time idling or thinking after you have set your goals.

(Miyamoto Musashi, "The Book of Five Rings", Trans. Kaufmann)

Are you procrastinating on your goal?

THURSDAY

I prayed for twenty years but received no answer until I prayed with my legs. (Attributed to Frederick Douglas)

How can you turn your prayers into action?

FRIDAY

The great thing in this world is not so much where we are, but in what direction we are moving.
(Oliver Wendell Holmes, "The Autocrat of the Breakfast Table")

In which direction are you moving?

SATURDAY / SUNDAY

Action is the proper fruit of knowledge.
(Thomas Fuller, "Gnomologia: Adagies and Proverbs")

Does your knowledge lead to action?

WEEK 41

MONDAY

Arriving at one goal is the starting point to another.
(Attributed to John Dewey)

What might be your next goal?

TUESDAY

I was taught that everything is attainable if you are prepared to give up, to sacrifice, to get it. (Stirling Moss, "All But My Life")

What will you sacrifice for your goal?

WEDNESDAY

It does not make any difference how beautiful your guess is. It does not make any difference how smart you are, who made the guess, or what his name is – if it disagrees with experiment it is wrong. (Richard P. Feynman, "The Character of Physical Law")

Will your goal work in the real world?

THURSDAY

Identify your Goals, Reality, and Options and come up with the best Way Forward for you in dealing with your personal issues.
(Alan Fine, "You Already Know How to Be Great")

Have you identified your Reality, Options, and Way Forward?

FRIDAY

You don't have to be a fantastic hero to do certain things – to compete. You can be just an ordinary chap, sufficiently motivated to reach challenging goals.
(Attributed to Sir Edmund Hillary)

Are you sufficiently motivated?

SATURDAY / SUNDAY

Some people don't like competition because it makes them work harder, better.
(Attributed to Drew Carey)

Are you afraid of competition? Why?

WEEK 42

MONDAY

An unequivocal end goal with an immovable deadline.
(David Nichols, "Return on Ideas")

Is your deadline immovable?

TUESDAY

Catch not at the shadow and lose the substance.
("Facts on File Dictionary of Proverbs")

Are you pursuing the shadow or the substance of your goal?

WEDNESDAY

The best topic statements focus outward on a specific customer need or service enhancement rather than focusing inward on some organizational goal. (Tom Kelly, "The Art of Innovation")

Is your goal focused outward? or inward?

THURSDAY

I dread success. To have succeeded is to have finished one's business on earth, like the male spider, who is killed by the female the moment he has succeeded in his courtship. I like a state of continual becoming, with a goal in front and not behind.
(George Bernard Shaw, "Yale Book of Quotations")

What goal is in front of you?

FRIDAY

There are no such things as unrealistic goals, only unrealistic time frames. (Canfield et al., "The Power of Focus")

What time frame is realistic for your goal?

SATURDAY / SUNDAY

He who begins much finishes little.
(German Proverb, "A Polyglott of Foreign Proverbs")

How many projects did you start this week?

WEEK 43

MONDAY

To strive actively to achieve some goal gives your life meaning and substance. (Bruce Lee, "Striking Thoughts")

Does your goal give your life meaning?

TUESDAY

A goal is not always meant to be reached. It often serves simply as something to aim at. (Bruce Lee, "Striking Thoughts")

Is your goal meant to be reached?

WEDNESDAY

Make at least one definite move daily toward your goal. (Bruce Lee, "Striking Thoughts")

What move did you make today?

THURSDAY

Keep your mind on the things you want and off those you don't.
(Bruce Lee, "Striking Thoughts")

What should you stop thinking about?

FRIDAY

Defeat simply tells me that something is wrong in my doing;
it is a path to success and truth.
(Bruce Lee, "Striking Thoughts")

How can you turn a recent defeat into success and truth?

SATURDAY / SUNDAY

The inability to adapt brings destruction.
(Bruce Lee, "Striking Thoughts")

How will you adapt to reach your goal?

WEEK 44

MONDAY

To the person with a firm purpose all men and things are servants.
(Attributed to Johann Wolfgang von Goethe)
Who and what will serve your goal?

TUESDAY

The proper function of man is to live, not to exist.
I shall not waste my days in trying to prolong them.
(Jack London, "Jack London's Tales of Adventure")
Does your goal inspire you to live? or allow you to exist?

WEDNESDAY

Control your own destiny or someone else will. (Jack Welch,
from "Control Your Destiny Or Someone Else Will"
by Tichy & Sherman)
Does this goal help you control your destiny?

THURSDAY

There is only one difference between a bad economist and a good one. The bad economist confines himself to the visible effect; the good one to both what can be seen and what must be foreseen. (Frederic Bastiat, "That Which is Seen, and That Which is Not Seen")

Have you foreseen the effects of your goal pursuit?

FRIDAY

When people are fanatically devoted to […] dogmas or goals, it's always because these dogmas or goals are in doubt. (Robert Prisig, "Zen and the Art of Motorcycle Maintenance")

Is your outcome in doubt?

SATURDAY / SUNDAY

If you want to be happy, set a goal that commands your thoughts, liberates your energy and inspires your hopes. (Attributed to Andrew Carnegie)

Does your goal command, liberate, and inspire you?

WEEK 45

MONDAY

In bocce, it is impossible to hit the target, yet without the target there is no game! Goals can be treated the same.
(Tim Hurson, Think Better)

How does your goal define the game you're playing?

TUESDAY

Goals help peoples keep their eyes on the vision.
(Kouzes & Posner, "The Leadership Challenge")

Is your goal explicitly tied to your vision of the future?

WEDNESDAY

Value-based goals are the most fulfilling type of goals to set.
(Thomas Leonard, "The Portable Coach")

What personal value is your goal tied to?

THURSDAY

Without clear goals, executive coaching relationships can become just a forum for rambling discussions about issues and an opportunity for the client to 'let off steam'. (Dembkowski & Eldridge, "The Seven Steps of Effective Executive Coaching")

Do you use goals to reduce rambling discussions?

FRIDAY

While ego-driven unrealistic goals might be temporarily motivating, it's not long before they're discouraging and expensive. (Marcum & Smith, "Egonomics")

Is your goal ego-driven?

SATURDAY / SUNDAY

Setting goals is a difficult intricate process. (Ordonez et al., 'Goals Gone Wild', hbswk.hbs.edu)

Have you set your goal carefully?

WEEK 46

MONDAY

Without dreams, without risks, only a trivial semblance of living can be achieved. (Mihaly Csikszentmihalyi, "Finding Flow")

Are you taking risks?

TUESDAY

Complexity requires investing psychic energy in goals that are new, that are relatively challenging.
(Mihaly Csikszentmihalyi, "Flow")

What challenging new goals do you have?

WEDNESDAY

The task undertaken has clear goals and provides immediate feedback. (Mihaly Csikszentmihalyi, "Flow")

Is your feedback immediate?

THURSDAY

As soon as the goals and challenges define a system of action, they in turn suggest the skills necessary to operate within it.
(Mihaly Csikszentmihalyi, "Flow")

Is it clear what skills you need?

FRIDAY

The balanced ratio between challenges and skills was recognized from the very beginning as one of the central conditions of the flow experience. (Mihaly Csikszentmihalyi, "Flow")

Are your skills equal to your challenge?

SATURDAY / SUNDAY

One prerequisite of flow is the ability to concentrate on goals without concern for anything irrelevant to the task. (Mihaly Csikszentmihalyi, "Good Business")

Have you removed the irrelevant from your schedule?

WEEK 47

MONDAY

Goal obsession is the force at play when we get so wrapped up in achieving the goal that we do it at the expense of a larger mission.
(Marshall Goldsmith, "What Got You Here Won't Get You There")

Are you obsessed with your goal?

TUESDAY

The complete goal of the ideal of organic architecture is never reached. Nor need be. What worthwhile ideal is ever reached?
(Frank Lloyd Wright, "An Autobiography")

Is your goal worth pursuing even if you don't reach it?

WEDNESDAY

All movements go too far.
(Bertrand Russell, "Unpopular Essays")

Are you at risk of going too far?

THURSDAY

Pleasure in learning, then, comes from the perception of progress toward a goal. (James Zull. "The Art of Changing the Brain")

Is your learning goal-oriented?

FRIDAY

Without the vision of a goal, a man cannot manage his own life much less the lives of others. (Genghis Khan, from "Genghis Khan and the Making of the Modern World" by Weatherford)

Can you manage yourself and others?

SATURDAY / SUNDAY

What does it matter that we take different roads so long as we reach the same goal? (Mahatma Gandhi, "Essential Gandhi")

Are you open to alternative paths to your goal?

WEEK 48

MONDAY

Of all the things I've done, the most vital is coordinating those who work with me and aiming their efforts at a certain goal. (Walt Disney, from "Walt Disney's Railroad Story" by Broggie)

Are you aiming the efforts of others at a goal?

TUESDAY

An effective goal focuses primarily on results rather than activity. (Steven R. Covey, "The 7 Habits of Highly Effective People")

Does your goal reward results? or activity?

WEDNESDAY

The ultimate judge of your swing is the flight of the ball. (Ben Hogan, from "Quotable Hogan")

What is the ultimate judge of your goal?

THURSDAY

We must understand that reaching our potential is more important than reaching our goals. (Brian Biro, "Beyond Success")

Is this goal challenging your potential?

FRIDAY

Writing strong goals is not easy.
(Wick et al., "The Six Disciplines of Breakthrough Learning")

Are you making time to write strong goals?

SATURDAY / SUNDAY

Man is pushed by drives. But he is pulled by values. He is always free to accept or reject a value he is offered by a situation.
(Viktor Frankl, "The Will to Meaning")

Is your goal pulled by values? or pushed by drives?

WEEK 49

MONDAY

It is in the interest of any human group to have its members working together toward the achievement of common goals.
(Robert Cialdini, "Influence")

Does your group or team have common goals?

TUESDAY

Is there a clear purpose for the meeting?
(Parker & Hoffman, "Meeting Excellence")

Do your meetings lack a clear purpose and goal?

WEDNESDAY

It is not enough to take steps which may some day lead to a goal; each step must be itself a goal and a step likewise.
(attributed to Johann Wolfgang von Goethe)

Have you made each step a goal?

THURSDAY

My definition of an executive's job is brief and to the point. It is simply this: Getting things done through other people. (Attributed to James Cash Penney)

Are you getting things done through others?

FRIDAY

The nicest thing about standards is that there are so many of them to choose from. (Attributed to Ken Olsen)

Are you making things clearer? or more confusing?

SATURDAY / SUNDAY

Management By Objectives works: if you know the objectives. 90% of the time you don't. (Peter Drucker, from "Guide to Management Ideas and Gurus" by Hindle)

Does everyone know the objectives?

WEEK 50

MONDAY

The only thing to worry about is the beginning.
("ABC Dictionary of Chinese Proverbs")
Do you know the first step in achieving your goal?

TUESDAY

Perfection of means and confusion of goals seem,
in my opinion, to characterize our age.
(Albert Einstein, "Out of My Later Years")
Are you more worried about 'how' than 'why'?

WEDNESDAY

None of us is a smart as all of us.
(Various)
Have you received input on your goal?

THURSDAY

Nothing can stop the man with the right mental attitude from achieving his goals; nothing on earth can help the man with the wrong mental attitude. (Attributed to Thomas Jefferson)

Do you have the right mental attitude?

FRIDAY

*I believe in myself and in my goals.
(Richard Branson, "Screw It, Let's Do It")*

Do <u>you</u> believe in yourself and your goals?

SATURDAY / SUNDAY

The victory of success is half won when one gains the habit of setting goals and achieving them. (Og Mandino, "The Greatest Salesman in the World II")

Is goal-setting a habit for you?

WEEK 51

MONDAY

The world judges with certainty.

(St Augustine of Hippo, "The Oxford Dictionary of Quotations")

Can your goals counter that certainty?

TUESDAY

We must learn when and how - pull the plug on people and ventures that do not serve our authentic goals and aspirations.

(Julia Cameron, "Walking in This World")

What can you pull the plug on?

WEDNESDAY

Better a flawed diamond than a perfect rock.

("ABC Dictionary of Chinese Proverbs")

Can you start the pursuit of your goal before it's perfect?

THURSDAY

Face reality as it is... not as it was or as you wish it to be.

(Jack Welch, "Winning")

Are you clear about your current state?

FRIDAY

It doesn't matter where you are coming from.
All that matters is where you are going.
(Brian Tracy, "Earn What You're Really Worth")

Are you clear about your destination?

SATURDAY / SUNDAY

Give me a stock clerk with a goal and I'll give you a man who will make history. Give me a man with no goals and I'll give you a stock clerk. (James Cash Penney, inc.com)

How will you make history?

WEEK 52

MONDAY

Specificity drives alignment. And vice-versa.

(Glenn Hughes, SMART as Hell)

Are you aligned?

TUESDAY

If it's rewarded or punished, it must be measured.

(Glenn Hughes, SMART as Hell)

Are you rewarded or punished without measurement?

WEDNESDAY

Aggressively Attainable goals are where the impact lies.

(Glenn Hughes, SMART as Hell)

Is your goal aggressively attainable?

THURSDAY

Relevance is first among equals.

(Glenn Hughes, SMART as Hell)

Is your goal relevant? To what?

FRIDAY

Time is not a destination. It's a source of energy for the journey.

(Glenn Hughes, SMART as Hell)

Are you using deadlines as a source of energy?

SATURDAY / SUNDAY

If your goals aren't SMART, your results probably aren't.

(Glenn Hughes, SMART as Hell)

How are your results?

Part Four

Smart as Hell Advice Resources

Make This Book Stronger!

SMART as Hell Advice is a living, evolving project. We invite you to co-create and co-design *SMART as Hell Advice* in the following ways:

1. *Distributed copy-editing.* If you find typographical or conceptual errors, please let us know. We work with on-demand publishing technology that enables us to immediately incorporate your corrections and improvements.
2. *Share your stories.* Send us the stories you have from your use of *SMART as Hell Advice.* Share big wins, horror stories, and small learning steps. If you're not sure how to tell your story, download the *Seven Sentence Story Template* from SMARTasHell.com.
3. *Contribute Tips.* Suggest additional pieces of advice based on your expertise and experience. We welcome your unusual and innovative ideas as well as traditional and tired-and-true ones.
4. *Provide a review.* We love to get your unbiased reviews of our books on Amazon, Barnes and Noble, or Goodreads.
5. *Request additional features.* If there are general additions – chapters, graphics, tools, worksheets, videos – that you would like to see incorporated in future editions, let us know.
6. *Suggest additional pieces of advice.* If you know of a quotation, maxim, proverb, or other words of advice that might be suitable for *SMART as Hell Advice II*, please forward it and get a free copy of the book if your suggestion makes the final cut.

And remember, your easiest one-stop contact is *info@SMARTasHell.com*

Get More SMART as Hell!

We've provided multiple ways to continue your *SMART as Hell!* experience:

- *Website*: SMARTasHell.com
- *Email*: info@SMARTasHell.com
- *YouTube*: YouTube.com/SMARTasHellVideo
- *Twitter*: twitter.com/SMARTasHell
- *LinkedIn:* Glenn Hughes
- *Pinterest*: pinterest.com/SMARTasHell/
- *Instagram*: instagram.com/glenn_hughes
- *Amazon Author Page*: amazon.com/author/ghughes
- *Goodreads*: goodreads.com/GlennHughes

- **SMART as Hell Workshops & Certification**: Contact *info@SMARTasHell.com* for live or virtual workshops.
- **SMART as Hell Video Training**: Subscribe, rent, or buy our videos at *SMARTasHell.pivotshare.com*
- **SMART as Hell Print Shop**: Teach and create SMART as Hell goals with posters, worksheets, and planners available at *marketplace.mimeo.com/SMART*
- **SMART as Hell Books**: Find all of the books in the SMART as Hell series at *SMARTasHell.com* or *Amazon.com*.
- **SMART as Hell Style**: Get *Photo Jolts!* shirts, mugs, mouse pads and more at *zazzle.com/smartashell*
- **Photo Jolts! and SMART as Hell Activity Decks**. *Photo Jolts!, Animal Jolts!, People Jolts!, Food Jolts!, Nature Jolts!, Poker Jolts! ArchiJolts!, SignJolts, Transport Jolts!, SMART as Hell Wisdom*, and *Photo Provocations* are available at *SMARTasHell.com*.

Table A: Advice Reflection

1. Write your goal.
2. Identify how much confidence you have that you can reach this goal, where 'Confident' equals 10 points and 'Skeptical' equals 0 points.
3. Identify how much desire you have to reach this goal, where 'Absolutely' equals 10 points and 'No Way' equals 0 points.
4. Select and silently read a quotation from the book. Jot down your immediate thoughts about the quotation.
5. Write the quotation in your own handwriting.
6. Do you notice anything different when you're writing the quote? What did you notice?
7. What about this quotation resonates with you? Underline those words or phrases. Why do these phrases resonate with you?
8. If the passage does not resonate with you, why not? What would you change to improve it?
9. Read the passage out loud to someone. Do you notice anything different when you're reading out loud? What do you notice?
10. Have you heard similar quotes, proverbs, or mantras? Write them down. Where did you read them?
11. Answer the provocation question that follows your goal. Capture any thoughts about your response.
12. What other questions does this quotation trigger?
13. How would you rewrite this quotation so that you 'own' it?
14. How does the quotation relate to your goal? Does it convince you that your goal is on target? Or that you need to change the goal? How? Why? Can you increase your confidence and desire?

Table B: SMART as Hell Goals

Make it Specific

Define, with a singular focus, in unambiguous language, who should do what and where it should be done.

Make it Measurable

Define clear start and finish lines, using a tracking system that can be trusted.

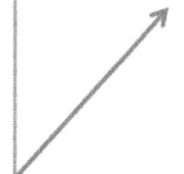

Make it Aggressively Attainable

Balance ability with aggressively SET challenges, defining upside and downside while accounting for prerequisites.

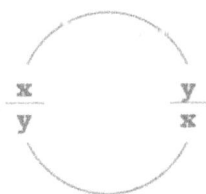

Make it Relevant

Define a 'why' that matters, and then satisfy that 'why' with minimal counterproductive impact.

Make it Time-bound

Set milestones and deadlines that win the race, by creating the appropriate energy and fluency.

ABOUT THE AUTHOR

Glenn Hughes is an award-winning author, photographer, facilitator, and learning leader. Glenn is Senior Director of Learning and Development at KLA-Tencor Corporation, a leading provider of process control and yield management solutions. KLA-Tencor's learning organization was recognized in 2008 as a charter member of TRAINING Magazine's *"Training Top 10 Hall of Fame"* after placing in the world's Top 10 Training Organizations for 5 consecutive years.

Glenn is also the founder of SMART as Hell, a company that helps individuals and organizations change their world one goal at a time. SMART as Hell develops best practices in goal writing and achievement – including the groundbreaking SMARTometer, a tool for measuring the effectiveness of goals.

Glenn's first book, *"Photo Jolts! Image-based Activities that Inspire Clarity, Creativity, and Conversation"* was co-written with interactive learning guru Sivasailam 'Thiagi' Thiagarajan. "Photo Jolts!" received The ISPI (International Society for Performance Improvement) 2014 Award of Excellence for Outstanding Human Performance Communication.

Glenn has received five Facilitation Impact Awards from the International Association of Facilitators, recognizing the world-class results that he and his clients have achieved. He is a frequent speaker at international conferences such as ATD (the Association for Talent Development), ISPI (the International Society for Performance Improvement), Lakewood's TRAINING Conferences, and the IAF (International Association of Facilitators).

Glenn lived in Asia for more than 10 years, working with many of the world's largest electronics companies while managing multi-million dollar operations in China, Singapore, and Japan. He holds a Master's Degree in Adult Education and Training and a Bachelor's Degree in Electronics Engineering Technology.

The SMART as Hell Library

Photo Jolts! Image-based Activities that Increase Clarity, Creativity, and Conversation
By Glenn Hughes & Sivasailam 'Thiagi' Thiagaragan
Foreword by Nancy Duarte
$29.99, Summer 2013

A Graphic Guide to Writing SMART as Hell Goals
Foreword by Sivasailam 'Thiagi' Thiagarajan
$24.99, Fall 2015

SMART as Hell Advice: A Year's Worth of Wisdom for Goal Achievement and Success
Foreword by Brent Bloom
$14.99, Fall 2015

The SMART as Hell Sessions: Four Conversations on the Art of Creating SMART Goals that Work
Foreword by Cal Wick
$24.99, Winter 2015

SMART as Hell: A Manifesto for Action, Alignment, and Achievement
$29.99, Spring 2016

The Rubrics Revolution: 200 Scorecards for Improving Personal and Professional Performance
$24.99, Spring 2016

MoVVeRRS: How Your SMART as Hell Mission, Vision, Values, Roles & Responsibilities, and Strategies Drive Energy, Engagement, and Execution
Foreword by Ed Muzio
$24.99, Summer 2016

The SMART as Hell Notebooks: A Right-Brain Guide to Great Goal-Setting
$19.99, Fall 2016

Contact Glenn at:

- SMARTasHell.com
- info@SMARTasHell.com

Find supplemental videos, worksheets, and links at:

http://smartashell.com/blog/SAHadvice

www.ingramcontent.com/pod-product-compliance
Lightning Source LLC
LaVergne TN
LVHW051606070426
835507LV00021B/2796